C000155984

The

MEVLIDI SHERIF

The Nativity of The Prophet Muhammad

Süleyman Chelebi

Translated by
F. Lyman MacCallum

The Ottoman Community and
Heritage Foundation Trust

British Library Cataloguing-in-Publication Data.
A catalogue record for this book is available from the British Library.

ISBN-10: 1916439306
ISBN-13: 978-1916439306

Originally published in 1943 by John Murray. This edition is published in 2018 by The Ottoman Community and Heritage Foundation Trust, registered charity in England and Wales No. 1057630. Registered office: Godbys Farm, Cricklade, Swindon, SN6 6HT. For more information visit www.rabbaniway.co.uk

In the days of Tamerlane (at the end of the 14th century) Süleyman Chelebi was one of the royal chaplains of Sultan Beyazid the Thunderbolt. When Tamerlane overthrew Beyazid, Süleyman found refuge as chief–priest of the Great Mosque at Bursa. There, he composed the MEVLIDI SHERIF (The Birth–Song of the Prophet) to confute a teaching that Muhammed was no greater than other Prophets. The poem survives after 500 years and is much loved by the people of Turkey. It is recited at times of thanksgiving and sorrow and on many special occasions. An authority on Turkey said recently: "No one can know what Muhammed means to the Turk, unless he is familiar with this poem."

— *F. Lyman MacCallum*

꧁

CONTENTS

Editor's Note

In the Name of God, the Merciful, the Compassionate.

In the age of tribulations across the globe, the need for guidance and tranquility has never been greater.

The Mevlidi Sherif is a classic poem in praise of God's final Prophet Muhammed ﷺ and has been recited for centuries at times of joy and grief.

Written in Turkey at the end of the 14th century, this poem served as a collection of sunni beliefs about the status of Muhammad in relation to all of creation, much of which has sadly been confused in the modern day.

We hope this work serves as a medium for the love of Muhammed and His teachings of peace and mercy.

F. Lyman MacCallum translated this work during his travels to Turkey and was published as part of "the wisdom of the East" series in 1943 by John Murray. No alterations to the original wording has been made in this edition.

Introduction

A POEM which has lived in the heart of a people for five hundred years, cannot be without merit. The *Magnificat* is perhaps the nearest English approach to such poetical longevity, but the ceremonial use of that song in English must fall well short of the five centuries. One or two carols are perhaps our only current poetry to have survived from those days. To us the English of Chaucer seems far away and strange, yet the Mevlidi Sherif, written by a contemporary of Chaucer, still speaks to the heart of the common people of Turkey.

The author, Süleyman was one of the earliest Ottoman poets. His grandfather was Sheyh Mahmud, a learned theologian, and member of one of the Dervish orders. Süleyman's father was a certain Ahmed Pasha, Grand Vizier under Sultan Murad I (A.D. 1359–1389) Süleyman had a place in the retinue of Prince Süleyman, the most distinguished son of that Sultan. He was also a recognised leader in the Halvati order of Dervishes having received the instruction and blessing of the celebrated Sheyh, Amir Sultan (d. A.D. 1439). Under Sultan Beyazid the Thunderbolt (A.D. 1389–1403), Süleyman was one of the court chaplains.

On the overthrow of the Thunderbolt by Timur the Lame (Tamer lane), Süleyman found asylum as chief Imam (priest) of the Great Mosque at Bursa, at that time the Turkish capital. Here his death took place in the year A.H. 825 (1421) and his tomb is still revered in that city.

Popular legend, supported by Turkish chroniclers, ascribes to the Mevlid the following origin. During Süleyman's intendency of the Great Mosque, a preacher, more zealous than instructed, preaching from the text "We make no distinction between any of his prophets" (Koran, II, 285), declared that the Prophet Muhammed was not to be more highly regarded than were other true prophets. An Arab in the congregation was so outraged that he did not rest until an ecclesiastical order for silencing the expositor had been obtained. But as the obstinate fellow persisted in his error, and was joined in it by a good pan of the citizens of Bursa, the Arab one day "fell upon the preacher before the mosque and slaughtered him as a butcher doth a sheep" (Latifi). In the excitement of these events, Süleyman is said to have composed a single couplet out of which soon grew the entire poem. This couplet,

"No death did Jesus die, but he ascended
To join with all Muhammed's loyal people,"

is not found in the present translation. Such is the legend of the poem's origin.[1]

Much more probable is the suggestion that it may have been composed by Süleyman at the request of the Sultan, or of the poet's friends, in order that there might be a Turkish poem in praise of the Prophet similar to the Arabic poems of this nature which had been popular for centuries. Special celebration of the Prophet's birthday were first instituted at Arbela in the year A.H. 604 (1208) by al–Malik Muzaffer al–Din Kökbüri, brother–in–law of Saladin. These celebrations included parades, torchlight processions and feasts, as well as the more ancient custom of chanting poems expressing the unique position of the Prophet. This innovation met with strong opposition from the more orthodox Muslims, for whom the cult of the Prophet seemed a complete contradiction of early Islam, while the celebrations themselves seemed highly imitative of the Christmas festivities of the Crusaders, their enemies. This opposition has continued in some form down to the twentieth century but joyous practice has proved stronger than dogmatic theory during all the intervening generations.

[1] E. J. W. Gibb, *A History of Ottoman Poetry*, vol. I, p. 225. London, 1909.

The Birth of the Prophet is still an annual popular festival throughout the entire Muslim world. These celebrations are said to have been introduced into Turkey in the year A.H. 996 (1589) by Sultan Murad III. This is almost two centuries after Süleyman wrote his Mevlid, but it is natural to suppose that during those two centuries the poem may have been chanted on the 12th of Rebi–ul–evel, the third month of the Muslim year, and on other suitable occasions, without the accompaniment of the secular displays introduced later.

The original copy of the poem is said to have been dated at Bursa in the year A.H. 812 (1409). It was entitled, *Vesilatun Nedjat* (The Means of Deliverance). The oldest MSS. now known are from a period almost two centuries later. Though each claims to be a true copy of the original, they vary greatly in length. Von Hammer and Smirnov give 600 couplets as the length of the poem. MSS. studied by Engelke varied between 360 and 630 couplets, while printed copies are usually under 300 couplets. The present English translation contains some 263 couplets, in which it follows the printed Turkish original.[1] This text omits the two sections, which deal with the death of the Prophet and of his faithful Fatima. These death scenes

[1]   Süleyman Dede, *Mevlidi Serif.* Ahmet Halit Kitaphanesi, Istanbul, 1931.

are not found in some of the old MSS., and in the public chanting of the poem the death of the Prophet is often omitted, while the death of Fatima is practically never given.

The present translation has not been planned as a critical study of an ancient classic; rather it is an attempt to open the barriers of language so that Western readers may enter into something of the emotional experience, which is the Turkish listener's inheritance. On the ground that the death scenes, missing from many MSS., may not be part of the original poem, and because they are not often used in public recitals, the translator has felt justified in omitting these sections.

The style of the poem to quote Gibb, "is very simple, without art of any kind. All the same, the work has, in great measure on account of this, a picturesque directness; while there is an artless charm in the naïve and childlike fashion in which the poet presents his marvels that is absent from the more laboured and pretentious productions of later imitators."

As the accounts of the birth of Jesus, as given by Matthew and Luke, form one of the richest spiritual treasures for the Christian, so it is the poem of Süleyman Chelebi, rather than any more authentic sources, which fills the Turkish mind with emotional content regarding the birth of Muhammed.

The poem consists of a number of sections or cantos, usually separated by a couplet and response, which serve as chorus. These sections are as follows:

I. A song of invocation and praise to Allah.
II. A brief request (always carefully observed in recitals) for prayers for the author, "Süleyman, the lowly".
III. A discourse on the 'Light of Muhammed', or the prophetic succession.
IV. The birth of Muhammed.
V. The 'Merhaba', a triumphant chorus of welcome to the new–born Prophet.
VI. Further recital of the marvels attending the birth.
VII. The miracles of the Prophet.
VIII. The 'Miradj', or heavenly journey of the Prophet.
IX. Concluding confession and prayer.

At public services the recital is brought to a close by a 'Douadji', or prayer leader, to whose crescendo of petition the congregation responds at almost every breath with fervent Amins.

The present English translation has been made in the "Mesnevi" metre employed by Süleyman Chelebi, which runs: Fă–i'–lă–tŭn, fă–i'–lă–tŭn fă–i'–lŭn. The rhymed couplets of the original are, in translation and mostly un–rhymed, since fidelity to the text would otherwise too often have been sacrificed on the altar of harmony.

For critical study of some of the Mevlid MSS. to be found in European libraries, the reader is referred to the thesis by Irmgard Engelke.[1] A charming account of a salon recital at about the beginning of the present century is to be found in Halide Edib's novel, *The Clown and His Daughter,* where this recital becomes a turning point in the fortunes of the chief character.[2] Mouradja d'Ohsson has left a remarkable description of the annual Mevlid service celebrated with imperial display in the mosque of Sultan Ahmed during the eighteenth century. It runs:

"The Mevlid is a festival which Murad III instituted in A.H. 996 (1589) in honour of the birthday of the Prophet. This solemnity is celebrated on the 12th of Rebi–ul–evel by a sermon, or rather a panegyric, on the life of the Prophet, on his miracles and on his death. This celebration is for the court only, not for the people. The ceremonies observed there, a mixture of religious practices and political display are far from the spirit of the public cult of Islam.

[1]   Irmgard Engelke, *Süleyman Tschelebis Lobgedichte auf die Geburt des Propheten.* Halle, 1926.

[2]   Halide Edib, *The Clown and His Daughter*, chap. 42. London, 1935.

"This Mevlid always takes place, as do the two Bayram feasts, in the mosque of Sultan Ahmed, owing to the convenience for the great retinue of the Sultan offered by the spaciousness of the Hippodrome just opposite. The service takes place at about ten o'clock, between the morning and midday *Namaz*. The various orders of state go to the mosque separately, each lord followed by the officers of his household or department. All wear semi–gala apparel, but the one who presents himself with the most pomp is the Kizlar Aghasi, the Chief of the Black Eunuchs of the Palace. This is the one day in the year on which he is permitted to appear in public with great display, for at other times he leaves the Palace only in the train of the Sultan on occasions when the latter goes publicly to the mosque. He takes precedence in this festival in his capacity of Inspector General of the sacred funds of the two cities of Arabia. On this day he leaves the Palace half an hour before the Sultan, and goes to the mosque with a numerous retinue, composed of the whole body of the Black Eunuchs and of the halberdiers, in uniform.

"The order and rank of the chief officers of state in the mosque are regulated on this occasion by a special etiquette. The Grand Vizier and the Mufti place themselves before the prayer–niche, the first on the right and the second on the left, both seated on high stools, like cushions. To the right of the Grand Vizier

are the High Admiral, the Agha of the Janis-
saries and the Minister of Finance, at the head
of all the clerks, who are ranged behind him
in order of rank. These officers form a long
file underneath the royal loge. Each is seated
on a little carpet of Barbary. To the left of the
Mufti are the Jurists of the first rank. This file is
continued underneath the pulpit by the lower
Jurists, who form a second parallel line as far
as the Kürsü, or throne of the preacher Sheyhs.
Behind this line is a third, formed by the pro-
fessors, all these men of law being seated on
cushions. Between the first two lines, which
enclose a long rectangle, are the Secretary of
State and the Chief Usher. Each is seated on a
rug, turned not towards the prayer–niche but
towards the royal loge.

The chief of the Emirs (descendants of the
Prophet) enjoys particular distinction on
these days ; he has a seat apart from the rest
of the Jurists, of whom he is also one of the
leading members. He sits under a green tent
erected near the throne of the Sheyhs, and
is surrounded by a band of his *chaushes*, all
equally Emirs, and wearing the green turban.
The Grand Master of Ceremonies and a private
officer of the Grand Vizier stand erect behind
this minister, their backs to the prayer–niche.
The *Zaghardji–bashi* and the *Samsondju–bashi*
(staff officers of the Janissaries), both wearing
their great ceremonial turbans, also stand near

the throne of the Sheyhs. Finally, all this court is separated from the people by two rows of Janissaries in plain uniform.

"It is in the midst of these that the Sultan appears at the mosque with his usual retinue, composed only of the officers of his household, all in semi–gala dress. At the moment when His Majesty enters the loge, which he always does by a hidden doorway, one of the first gentlemen of his chamber announces his arrival by drawing aside the curtains. At this all the assembly stands, the Grand Vizier and Mufti take several steps towards the loge, and at the moment when the Sultan allows a portion of his head, or rather of his turban, to appear, these two make him a deep obeisance, and as the curtains close at the same instant, they resume their seats, as does everyone else.

"The ceremony begins with a panegyric divided into three parts, which are given successively by three priests: (1) by the chief priest of the mosque of Aya Sophia, as the first of all the preachers of the royal mosques; (2) by the chief priest of the mosque wherein the ceremony is taking place; and (3) and by the chief priest of one of the other royal mosques, which enjoy this distinction in turn annually, according to the rank of the mosque. During the panegyric, the Swordbearer and the First Valet de Chambre, who are the first gentlemen of the Sultan's chamber, present him during the discourse of each of the three Sheyhs, with sherbet, with rose–water and with perfume of aloes–wood. At the same time, sixty of the *Zuluflu–baltadjis*, officials of the Palace, perform the same honours thrice for the assembled Jurists and officials. As each of the three Sheyhs finishes his discourse and descends from the throne, he is received at the foot of the ladder by the chief Secretary and the Steward of the Halberdiers, two important officers of the Palace under the Chief of the Black Eunuchs. As a special honour they support these priests under the arms, and decorate them with a robe of sable fur in the name of the Sultan.

"At the end of the panegyric, the Muezzins of the mosque intone from the height of their tribune the *Nathi–sherif*, a hymn in praise of the Prophet. Fifteen other singers called Muveshis, seated behind the movable platform erected only for this ceremony, then sing one of the chants (*Ilahi*). After that, three ministers called *Mevlid–Hanan*, mount the platform and chant successively the Mevlid, a kind of hymn on the birth of the Prophet, in Turkish verse. Then the *Baltadjis* of the Palace, to the number of two hundred, advance carrying huge trays in their hands. These are loaded, some with sweetmeats, others with ten or twelve crystal or porcelain vases filled with sherbets of different kinds and colours. The *Zaghardji–bashi* and *Samsondju–bashi* immediately leave their places, and with their own hands place two of the trays before the Grand Vizier, and others before the Mufti. The administrators and clerks of the sacred funds of the two cities of Arabia advance at the same time to present two of these trays to each of the Jurists and the officers of state who make up the assembly. Nothing is richer than the trays destined for the Sultan; the Swordbearer alone has the right to place them before His Majesty.

"As soon as the first of the three singers has finished the first section of the Mevlid hymn, he descends from the platform and gives place to the second, who continues. At the moment when this one pronounces the words which tell of the birth of the Prophet, the whole assembly stands, and they proceed to the ceremony of receiving the official letter sent to the Sultan by the Sherif of Mecca. This letter is in answer to one, which His Majesty addresses annually to the Prince of Arabia on the subject of the safety of pilgrims, and of the other different matters relating to the pilgrimage.

"The Sultan's letter is put into the hands of the *Surra–Emini* the day he leaves Constantinople with the sacred revenues for Mecca; the reply of the Sherif is confided to the *Müdjdedji–bashi*, who, returning to Damascus with the Pasha of that province and the pilgrim caravan, always takes care to reach Constantinople a few days before the celebration of the Mevlid. On this day, this officer stands in the mosque beside the halberdiers, dressed in a robe and wearing a turban wrapped round with black muslin and crowned with a plume. At the invitation of the private officer of the Grand Vizier, who leaves his place for this purpose, this deputy approaches, holding high in his hand the letter of the Sherif, enclosed in a purse of green satin, and presents it to the Grand Vizier. The First Minister passes it to the Secretary of State, who with a grave step, and preceded by the chief of the ushers, approaches the loge of the Sultan. The Chief of the Black Eunuchs receives the letter at the door of the loge and presents it to the Sultan. The latter returns it to him after reading it ; the Chief of the Black Eunuchs passes it back to the Secretary of State, to be deposited according to custom in the Imperial Chancery.

"At this moment the Chief of the Black Eunuchs is honoured with a sable robe which he dons in the Sultan's presence. In his turn this official gives robes of honour to the Secretary of State and the three officials. Throughout this ceremony the chanting of the Mevlid continues. Immediately the hymn is finished, the three singers or *Mevlid–Hanan* also receive a robe of honour each. The service concludes with a brief prayer by all the assembly.

"Then the two general officers of the Janissaries approach the Grand Vizier and the Mufti, remove the trays from in front of them and pass them to their own footmen, to be carried to

these officers' quarters as a perquisite. The ser-
vants of the Jurists and other lords do the same,
causing a general movement in the mosque.

"The Sultan returns to the Palace with the
same retinue. As on other feast days, he bestows
money on the people ; the First Valet de Cham-
bre throws silver money to the crowd. Neither
the Grand Vizier nor any other official follows
the Sultan to the Palace. Even the Chief of
the Black Eunuchs does not accompany him.
This official returns a quarter of an hour after
His Majesty. On leaving the mosque he is
accompanied by the Agha of the Janissaries,
who walks before his horse for a distance of
not less than fifty paces. All the expense of this
festival, which is held to honour the Chief of
the Black Eunuchs, is paid from the revenues of
this mosque, under the oversight of the Voivode
of Galata, acting in his capacity as responsible
guardian. He has for the expenses of this cer-
emony a fixed allowance of 7500 piasters (L.
stg. 1,700).

"This festival is celebrated in other mosques
as well, but on different days, though usually
during the course of this or the succeeding
month. The celebration is always at the will of
the responsible guardian of each mosque, who
arranges the day with the *Yazidji–Effendi*, and
with the clerks and officials of the Department
of Sacred Endowments, under the inspection
of the Chief of the Black Eunuchs. They alone

attend the festival, which in other mosques is always celebrated without any particular display and with few ceremonies."[1]

The following translation of a deed establishing a fund for the regular chanting of the Mevlid for the repose of the souls of a slave and of her mistress may also be of some interest:

"In the year 1232 (1816/17) the very virtuous and charitable Dame Mihri Vefa, through her *hala*, El Nadji Reyhan Aga, and in the presence of the Head Confectioner (of the Palace), hath given the sum of 2000 piasters to the confectionery kitchens in order that prayers may be said for the repose of the soul of Dame Durnab, slave of Sultan Mahmud II, and also for the repose of the soul of the giver. The interest from this sum is to be expended for the reading of the Mevlid and for contingent expenses as follows:

"60 piasters for 10 okes of 'kalbe' (candy); 60 piasters for 12 okes of mixed candies; 2 piasters for one oke of rose–water; 15 piasters for 15 drams of sandal–wood; 10 piasters for one oke of coffee; 15 piasters for the 1st Reader of the Mevlid; 5 piasters for the 2nd Reader; 2 piasters each for five large kerchiefs; 10 piasters for the head confectioner; 6 piasters for a

---

[1]   Mouradja d'Ohsson, *Tableau général de l'empire ottoman*, vol. II, pp. 358-368. Paris, 1799-1824.

2nd official from the confectionery kitchens; 4 piasters for each of 3 others; 3 piasters for two others; and 4 piasters for the person in charge of the arrangements. The administrator of this Vakif must be bonded. May Allah pardon the sins and reward the good deeds of those who preserve this trust. Amin."

In Republican Turkey the Mevlid continues to be chanted in mosques and in homes, and the recital takes place either on some religious festival, such as the Night of Power, or at a time of rejoicing, such as a house–warming or a victory of the Turkish arms, or at a time of mourning. Perhaps its commonest occurrence is on the fortieth day after a death; invitations to such memorial recitals are a common feature of the Istanbul press. During the recital rose–water is sprinkled on the hands of the congregation, and sweets are distributed.

The fact that the Mevlidi Sherif, as the finest expression of reverence for Muhammed, forms an essential part in the religious pattern of most Turkish minds, and that from its striking pictures and musical lines many Turks draw a large part of their stock of religious ideas, may give this poem interest and significance even for many who have little direct contact with the world of Islam. Remembering what the music of Christmas carols means to the Western world may help to an understanding of what the Turk experiences as he listens to the music of Süleyman Chelebi's Mevlidi Sherif.

The Mevlidi Sherif

In the Name of God, the Merciful, the Compassionate.

Allah! This name invoke we in beginning,
For this is ever due from us, his servants.

Allah! The name which brings to all who call it,
God's present aid, the weight of labour light'ning.

Did Allah's name begin each fresh endeavour,
The end would ne'er fall short of full attainment.

With every breath repeat that name, unceasing;
In Allah's name see every task completed.

Who says: Allah! in language truly loving
Shall see his sins, like autumn leaves, removing.

That man is pure who on the pure name calleth;
Who cries: Allah! attains his every purpose.

Come then in love, that holy name repeating;
Your woeful tears and heartfelt fears commingle.

He may accord us mercy, that great Sov'reign,
The Generous, the Merciful, the Holy.

He's One! Doubt not his Unity eternal,
Though multitudes profess their creeds of error.

While yet the worlds were not, Allah had being,
Mighty was he, richer than all creation.

He was, while yet was found nor man nor angel,
No earth, moon, sun, nine spheres nor highest heaven.

His was the art by which these all were founded,
Him they confess, his Unity they witness.

Omnipotence in these revealed his power
While giving proofs that testified his Oneness.

"Be!" said he, and the world stood forth in splendour;
Were he to say: "Be not!" so would it vanish,

Why, therefore, need we still prolong discussion?
Allah is One; beyond him is none other.

The proofs might be till Judgement Day extended—
Yea, more such Days might fall ere they were ended.

Since Muhammed is cause of this existence,
With simple hearts petition his assistance.

If from Hell's flame you hope to find salvation,
With grief and love repeat the Salutation.

Response

Blessing and greeting upon thee, O Apostle of Allah!
Blessing and greeting upon thee, O Beloved of Allah!

Introduction

O worthy friends, ere we begin our story,
We charge you with a legacy most solemn;

A charge which he who holds in due observance,
Musk–sweet shall be his soul among its fellows.

May God Most High remember with his mercy
Each one of you who me[1] in prayer remembers.

For me, your slave, make earnest supplication;
A Fatiha I beg, your rich donation.

The Fatiha

Praise be unto Allah, the Lord of all creatures, the Most Merciful, the King of the Day of Judgement. Thee do we worship and of Thee do we beg assistance. Direct us in the right way, the way of those to whom Thou hast been gracious; not of those against whom Thou are incensed, nor of those who go astray. Amin.

[1]   *I.e.* the soul of the author, Süleyman.

The Prophetic Succession

When man was first by Allah's pow'r created,
  The ornament was he of all things living.

To Adam came all angels in submission,
  A gesture oft, at God's command, repeated.

On his brow first God set the Light of Prophets.
  Saying: This Light belongs to my Belovèd.

Long years that Light shone there, nor ever wavered,
  Until the prophet's earthly life was ended.

Know that to Eve's brow next the Light migrated,
  Remaining there through many months and seasons.

Then Seth received this sigil of Mustafa,[1]
  Which glowed more bright as year to year was added.

Thus Abraham and Ishmael received it—
  My time would fail should all the line be counted.

From brow to brow, in linkèd chain unbroken,
  The Light at last attained its goal, Muhammed.

---

[1] Throughout this poem the names Ahmed, Muhammed and Mustafa are used for the Prophet.

*The Mercy of the Worlds appeared, and straightway
To him the Light took wing, its journey ended.*

*Give ear, then, to his merits, O ye pious,
And know who is the one will justify us.*

*If from Hell's flame you hope to find salvation,
With love and zeal repeat the Salutation.*

Response

*Blessing and greeting upon thee, O Apostle of Allah!
Blessing and greeting upon thee, O Beloved of Allah!*

The Birth of Muhammed
(on whom be peace!)

Now Amine, Muhammed's tender mother
(Mother–of–pearl, her one pearl like none other),

Had been with child by Abdullah, the faithful,
And time had sped, her hour was fast approaching.

But in that night when he to earth descended,
A host of herald signs bespoke his coming.

It was the happy month, Rebi–ul–evel,
And of this month the twelfth, Isneyn, the Blessed,

On which was born the Welfare of the Peoples,
'Mid marvels by his wond'ring mother witnessed.

"I saw," said she, "a wondrous light up–springing,
And streaming from my house, with blaze increasing.

Round it the sun revolved, moth–like and dazzled,
While earth and sky gave back this
matchless splendour.

Heaven's radiant doors stood wide, and Dark
was vanquished.
There came three angels bearing shining banners;

They raised one at the world's east brink, another
At farthest west, the third atop the Kaaba.

Then rank on rank the heavenly host descended,
And round my dwelling marched, as 'twere
God's mansion.

This multitude made clear to me that straightway
Their lord to earth would come, to bless his people.

In air I saw a silken mattress wafted,
By angel band adoringly attended.

So clear before my eyes appeared these visions,
That all my heart o'erflowed with glowing wonder.

But now the wall at hand was sharply riven;
In stepped three shining houris[1] fresh from Heaven.

Some say that one was Asiye, fair consort
Of Egypt's King, who noble Moses nurtured.

One was, without a doubt, the lady Mary;
The third, a graceful houri, their attendant.

Most graciously the moon–browed three
approached me,
And, bowing low, said kindly: 'Peace be on thee!'

[1] Angelic, heavenly beings.

Then close at hand they sat in friendly circle
While each announced glad tidings of Mustafa.

To me they said: 'Not since the world's creation
Hath mother had such cause for exultation.

No son like thine, such strength and grace possessing,
Hath God to earth sent down, for its redressing.

Great favour hast thou found, thou lovely mother,
To bear a son surpassing every other.

Sultan is he, all hidden truth possessing,
Full knowledge of the Unity professing.

For love of him, thy son, the skies are turning;
Mankind and angels for his face are yearning.

This is the night foretold in song and story,
In which the worlds rejoice to see his glory.

This night the world a paradise he maketh,
This night God's mercy on mankind awaketh.

Men of goodwill this night are all elated,
All upright men this night have long awaited.

The Mercy of both Worlds is he, Mustafa,
The Refuge of the sinner is Mustafa!'

With gracious words his nature thus they pictured,
And for that blessèd Radiance set me yearning."

Here Amine made ending, for the hour
In which should come that best of men had sounded.

"I thirst," she cried, "I thirst, I burn with fever!"
A brimming glass to her at once was proffered.

White was that glass, than snow more white,
and colder;
No sweetmeat ever made held half such sweetness.

"I drank it, and my being filled with glory,
Nor could I longer self from light distinguish.

On pinions bright a bird of white came floating,[1]
And stroked my back, so strongly yet how kindly;

The Sultan of the Faith that hour was given,
And drowned in glory lay both earth and heaven."

Now pray to him, make peace and full submission,
That Paradise be yours for your contrition.

If from Hell's flame you hope to find salvation,
With love and zeal repeat the Salutation.

[1]   At this point in the recital the congregation
stands to welcome the arrival of the Prophet.

Response

Blessing and greeting upon thee, O Apostle of Allah!
Blessing and greeting upon thee, O Beloved of Allah!

All things created joyfully acclaimed him,
Sorrow was done, new life the world was flooding.

The very atoms joined in mighty chorus,
Crying with sweetest voices: Welcome, welcome!

Welcome, O matchless Sultan, thou art welcome,
Welcome, O Source of Knowledge, thou art welcome.

Welcome, thou Secret of the Koran, welcome,
Welcome, Affliction's Cure, thou art most welcome.

Welcome, thou Nightingale of Beauty's garden,
Welcome, to him who knows the Lord of Pardon.

Welcome, thou Moon and Sun of God's salvation,
Welcome, who knowst from Truth no deviation.

Welcome, the rebel's only place of hiding,
Welcome, the poor man's only sure confiding.

Welcome, Abiding Spirit, thou art welcome,
Welcome, the Lovers' Cup–bearer, O welcome.

Welcome, thou Eyesight of thy true adorer,
Welcome, thou Prince, loved by the World's Restorer.

Welcome, the humble soul's Illuminator,
Welcome, thou cherished Friend of the Creator.

Welcome, thou Soul Belovèd, thou art welcome,
Welcome, Affliction's Cure, thou art most welcome.

Welcome, since thou of both worlds art the Blesser,
Welcome to thee, the sinner's Intercessor.

Welcome, thou Monarch by two worlds awaited,
For whom both earth and heaven were created.

O thou, whose face with noonday splendour gloweth,
Whose hand is quick to raise up all the fallen,

Thou art the stay and comfort of all lovers,
The only refuge both of slave and freeman;

O balm of broken hearts, joy of the contrite,
O Sultan of the world and all its creatures,

King art thou to the noble race of Prophets,
Light–of–the–eye to men, both saint and simple;

O, last to mount the throne of the Apostles,
O thou, the seal and warrant of the Prophets,

Whose light did make the whole world shine
in brilliance,
Whose rose–like beauty filled the world with roses,

O'ercame the night of ignorance and error,
And brought Attainment's Vineyard to perfection,

O thou, Belov'd of God, grant thy assistance,
Smile on us in that hour when ends existence.

If from Hell's flame you hope to find salvation,
With love and zeal repeat the Salutation.

Response

Blessing and greeting upon thee, O Apostle of Allah!
Blessing and greeting upon thee, O Beloved of Allah!

When he, the Friend of God ruthful and clement,
Brought to the world the beauty of his presence,

Each angel to his fellow bore glad tidings,
While earth itself in exultation trembled.[1]

---

[1]   A reference to the earthquake believed to have taken place at the time of the Prophet's birth. In this earthquake the famous vaulted hall at Ctesiphon is supposed to have been ruined.

Affrighted by these portents, sweet Amine
'Twixt swoon and waking saw a wondrous vision—

She found herself alone, the houris vanished,
Likewise her son. Believing that they had him,

In tremulous dismay her loss she pondered,
Imploring God the while to send him to her.

Her anxious eye sought every nook and corner,
Till suddenly she spied him, deep in worship;

The Welfare of Mankind, facing the Kaaba,
Had fallen prone, in holy adoration.

There he with head and tongue was praising Allah,
Whose Unity his outstretched finger witnessed.

He cried: "Oh God, I look to thee, beseeching,
Grant me my people, let them all be near me!"

Amine said: "So clear I saw this vision,
That I to earth was drawn by my impatience.

So my mind cleared, these shadows all departed,
And lo, my son, light of my eyes, Mustafa!

But hear the marvel—cord already severed,
Eyes painted, and his circumcision perfect!

His face was lighted with a smile like daybreak,
A sight which set my heart with joy a–tremble.

My heart glowed hot with fires of tender passion,
I snatched him up, and pressed him to my bosom.

Trembled his lips, I saw that words were forming.
What could my Bird of Paradise be saying?

I bent my ear towards his mouth and listened
With wonder, for his speech was plain to follow.

Freely submitting all his will to Allah,
He murmured low: 'My people, oh, my people!'"

For you he prayed, though he was but an infant,
Yet you, full–grown, forsake his path of virtue.

'My people!' thus he yearningly addressed you ;
Salute him then, for love will heal and rest you.

If from Hell's flame you hope to find salvation,
With love and zeal repeat the Salutation.

Response

Blessing and greeting upon thee, O Apostle of Allah!
Blessing and greeting upon thee, O Beloved of Allah!

The Miracles of Allah's Apostle

That night the Meccan chiefs, men pure and guileless,
While circling round the Kaaba, deep in worship,

Beheld the shrine in homage bow its summit,
And right itself again, not one stone missing.

At this each noble chief his neighbour greeted,
Crying: "The Welfare of Mankind is with us!"

And how the Kaaba spoke with voice of triumph;
"Tonight is born the Sun, who all men lighteth.

From idols and all blasphemy he'll cleanse me,
And save from those who hold that God
hath partners.

Henceforth his people, pure of heart and lowly,
Round me will march barefoot, with
heads uncovered!"

That night the Prophet's thund'rous drums resounded,
Satan that night from heaven was ejected;

In shrine and temple dashed were god and painting,
While 'neath God's scourge the sons of wrath
were fainting.

If from Hell's flame you hope to find salvation,
With love and zeal repeat the Salutation.

RESPONSE

Blessing and greeting upon thee, O Apostle of Allah!
Blessing and greeting upon thee, O Beloved of Allah!

The Glory of the World, when he was forty,
Assumed the crown of prophecy, mysterious.

Oft heard he then a great voice cry: "O Faithful,
Thee have I made to be the world's sure Mercy!"

By verse and verse came down the sacred Koran,
While miracles most passing strange were witnessed.

Know first that never did that sacred body
Cast shadow on the earth, not e'en at noonday;

From head to foot his frame was light in essence,
And sure it is that light has not a shadow.

Above that noble head there hung unfailing,
A cloudy fragment sent from heav'n to shield him;

Its shadow cooled the burning heats of summer,
And where he moved, the cloud to him was faithful.

The miracles his eyes displayed are many;
Attend, while I recount these blessed marvels.

Whate'er those eyes might see before them lying,
Could they behold as clear when left behind him.

When Gabriel brought down a revelation,
The very instant when from heav'n he parted,

On earth his scent would fill the Prophet's nostrils,
Who waited then with joy the coming message.

Those glorious lips had but to quiver faintly,
And lo, the sun with all his train would tremble.

When winds of dawn about his head played lightly,
The scent of musk and amber filled their eddies.

By night his pearly teeth so brightly glittered,
Lost needles by that light might be recovered.

His breast poured forth a light by which his comrades
Through darkest night could walk the path of safety.

The Friend of God in twain the moon divided,
Though he but gestured towards it with his finger.

The Ruler of the World would oft plant palm-trees,
And pluck the honeyed fruit within the hour.

This tale might be till Judgement Day extended—
Yea, more such Days might fall ere it were ended.

If from Hell's flame you hope to find salvation,
With love and zeal repeat the Salutation.

Response

Blessing and greeting upon thee, O Apostle of Allah!
Blessing and greeting upon thee, O Beloved of Allah!

The Heavenly Journey of Allah's Apostle

Come hither, ye who long to feel love's fires,
Who count yourselves true lovers of the Loved One.

Come, hear how he one night to heav'n ascended;
And burn with love the while, if ye be lovers.

Upon a Thursday night, and this is certain,
For this became th' illustrious Night of Power,[1]

Our Lord, the royal child of noble fortune,
At home was resting in the cool of evening.

While thus in high–souled ease he was there seated,
To Paradise[2] God sent his angel saying:

"Take thence a belt of rank, a crown well–jewelled,
A trusty chestnut steed of noble breeding,

Lead him to my Belovèd for his service,
To visit highest heaven and behold me."

---

[1]   The 27th night in the month of Ramazan.
[2]   Lowest of the heavenly spheres.

So Gabriel to Paradise descended,
And saw that countless horses there were grazing.

But in their midst stood one with eyes right tearful,
Who would nor eat nor drink, so mournful was he.

His sorrowing eyes streamed like the flooded Jeyhan,
Pining and grief his woeful heart had melted.

Said Gabriel: "Why weep you so, what ails you,
What wounds are these your soul and body carry?

Your comrades all do graze and drink or wander,
While you stand moaning; say, what do you long for?"

He answered: "Forty thousand years, O Master,
Not food or drink, but love my frame has nourished.

For, once, my ear was drawn by sudden music,
Voices divinely sweet, low, but heart–piercing,

Which sang in lovely unison: 'Muhammed!'
Since then I know not what strange mood is on me,

My left from right can I not now distinguish;
The Master of that name I love for ever.

Within my breast my heart is lean with longing;
Not sight but only sound has made me love him.

This yearning makes of Paradise a prison,
By night and day these groans and sighs I utter.

Though to the eye I seem to stand in heaven,
The pangs of absence are my endless torment.

Him must I find, whose glorious name I cherish,
Or else this frame incontinent must perish!"

Cried Gabriel: "O matchless steed celestial,
Languish no more, for God your prayer has answered.

Whoever bears love's emblems in his body
Shall know, some day, the joy of lovers' meeting.

Come now to meet your loved one as appointed,
With healing balm your heart shall be anointed."

The steed and Gabriel set forth together,
And soon appeared before the body Prophet.

"Hail Mustafa! We bring salaams from Allah,
Who sends you earnest wishes for your welfare.

He bids you come and be his guest in heaven,
To gaze upon its wonders and behold him.

Unsealed tonight is God's long-hidden secret;
Revealed tonight, to you alone, his visage.

Filled are both worlds tonight with flooding Zemzem[1];
And angels fly with tidings of your coming;

The eight firm gates of heav'n they now have opened,
And scatter, free, rich blessings o'er creation.

The abodes of bliss and spirits blest await you;
Come then with us, Mustafa, to the Eternal.

Behold, this steed from Paradise I brought you,
To prove it was our Lord himself besought you."

At once Mustafa rose to do his bidding,
And donned with joy the crown which they provided.

The angel held the steed while Ahmed mounted,
And settled firm astride the beast celestial.

Before him went their guide, the way to open;
The chestnut spread his wings and soared
towards heaven.

In that same breath, the Sultan of the Nations
Dismounted in Jerusalem the Sacred.

There, souls of prophets came straightway to greet him,
Each seeking means to do him signal honour.

[1] Water of the Zemzem well in the sacred enclosure at Mecca.

At this a cry from Allah reached the spirits,
Bidding them follow Mustafa in worship.

The Welfare of Mankind then sought the prayer-niche,
While souls in rows behind joined in the Namaz,[1]

Two rek'ats[2] they performed, there on the Aksa,[3]
The order of the Will Supreme obeying.

A ladder now appeared, of light constructed ;
And by its rungs their journey they continued.

Till wond'ringly he stood at last in heaven ;
The Bird of Paradise its wide gate entered.

He saw the heavenly citizens at worship,
Engaged each one in reverent devotions.

Some sang the names of God, some spoke his glory ;
Here beads were told, there holy praises shouted ;

Some prostrate lay in humble adoration.
Some stood erect, some bowed to earth their faces,

[1]   The act of worship prescribed five times daily for Muslims.

[2]   One of the cycles of prayer and genuflexion which are repeated in the *Namaz*.

[3]   The enclosure surrounding the mosque of Omar on the site Solomon's temple at Jerusalem.

Some by the love of God were so enraptured,
That lost they were in dream, or trance ecstatic.

These citizens all hurried towards Mustafa,
Intent to show respect and pay him homage.

Congratulating him upon his journey,
They said: "Thou art most welcome, O Muhammed,

Our Intercessor in the Day of Judgement!
The crown of bliss tonight thy brow encircles;

Wander at will throughout the storeyed heavens,
And share tonight our Sultan's conversation,

An honour ne'er before to man accorded,
For none was worthy thus to be exalted."

That night the Prophet roamed, led on by passion,
To view the spheres with comprehending glances.

From each he garnered store of hidden wisdom,
Until his steps approached the bourn of Sidre,[1]

Beyond which point had Gabriel not ventured
Since first the spheres to order were subjected.

---

[1] A tree in the seventh heaven. Also the mansion of the Angel Gabriel.

When Gabriel made sign he could no further,
The Mercy of the Worlds declared in sadness:

"These paths I know not, all is blank before me;
A stranger I, how shall I go without thee?"

At this the angel cried: "Prophet belovèd,
Think not thyself to be e'en here a stranger!

For thee alone these spheres have been created,
With men and jinns, the houris and bright angels.

But here my range doth end, here is my border,
Nor know I what beyond this frontier lieth.

It is commanded by our glorious Master,
That I nor wing nor heart beyond this venture.

Should I transgress, swift as the lightning flashes
The fire of God would smite my bones to ashes."

The Glory of the World to this made answer:
"Stay thou within the pale, as is commanded.

But I, whose steps hath Love to this point guided,
I must go on, although at once I perish.

Who presses on, in death's despite, unshrinking,
Shall see his love, and stand, those features drinking.

Count not the way of love adverse or winding;
To yield the head may prove the surest finding."

If from Hell's flame you hope to find salvation,
With love and zeal repeat the Salutation.

RESPONSE

Blessing and greeting upon thee, O Apostle of Allah!
Blessing and greeting upon thee, O Beloved of Allah!

While thus he was with Gabriel conversing,
Refref [1] appeared and, bowing, bade him follow.

The Sultan of the World and he together
Set forth from Sidre for their destination.

Soon came a chasm, abysmal and upreaching,
Where's neither sky, nor earth, nor habitation;

This boundless space is neither full nor empty,
Its qualities escape man's comprehension.

---

[1]   There is uncertainty among the commentators as to what *Refref* represents. Some suppose it to be a heavenly beast not unlike the *Burak* which had carried the Prophet during the first stage of his heavenly journey.

Before they found the seat of the Eternal.
Full seven times ten thousand veils were lifted.

When each was raised, a solemn voice commanded:
"Approach, my friend; delay not to come hither!"

He saw and crossed those empyrean spaces,
And stood at last before the Lord Almighty.

There Majesty revealed to the Belovèd,
In fullest light, six aspects of his Beauty.

He saw the Lord of Glory full and clearly,
As will his followers in the World Hereafter.

The King communed with Mustafa, 'tis certain,
Though neither word, nor voice, nor sign were needed.

"I am your heart's desire," he said, "your solace,
Your only love, the only God you worship.

For me by night and day you sigh, unceasing,
And say: 'Why may I not behold his beauty?'

Come Friend, the love I feel for you is boundless,
To you I give all people for your bondsmen.

Whatever you desire shall now be granted;
For every ill a thousand cures stand ready."

Then answered Mustafa: "O God of Mercy,
Veiler of Faults, most graciously forgiving,

What shall become of these thy halting people,
How shall they find their way into thy presence?

By day and night their deeds compass rebellion;
I fear lest the Abyss should be their portion.

O Majesty, this is my sole petition—
My people, may they be by thee accepted."

From Truth Supreme a loving cry resounded:
"I grant them all to you, my friend, Muhammed!

Your people now to you have I accorded;
My Paradise I promise for their portion.

O Friend, was such a trifle worth the asking?
Since you now have my love, my gentle Lover,

Would you make suit for this rebellious handful?
You might have asked both worlds for your possessing.

You are the glass which mirrors my reflection;
Your name have I inscribed with mine together."

God said moreover: "Well I know, my Prophet,
That gazing thus your soul will ne'er feel surfeit;

But go, and give my slaves my invitation
To come and gaze at will upon my features.

You came to heav'n and for them interceded;
Your people shall approach me in the Namaz.

Whenever one performs the Namaz duly,
It wins him merit like to those in heaven.

All forms of worship are in it included;
It is both way to God and sure arrival.

Those faithful souls who pay it five times daily
Shall God reward as though they had done fifty."

This conversation lasted but an instant,
Though ninety thousand words were in it spoken.

In that same breath, the world's great Prince and Sultan
Was back once more, under the roof familiar.

To his revered companions he narrated,
From first to last, the story of his journey.

They said: "Oh thou to whom we turn our faces,
Blessed be thine exalted, heavenly journey!

We all are slaves, thou art our glorious ruler
In all our hearts thou art the full–moon shining.

Enough for us the call to be thy nation ;
Enough if we may win thine approbation."

The Petition

So come, let us confess our sad rebellions;
With secret moan and bitter groan repenting.

Though life should last however many seasons,
Death shall one day become our sole employment.

So let us now defeat death's pangs and sadness,
By evermore entreating: God forgive us!

Our deeds have ever been of God unworthy;
We know not what may be our last condition.

Our worthless course have we not left nor altered
No preparations made for life eternal.

Our names we make to shine before the people,
But secretly our hearts we all have tarnished.

Each breath sees us commit sins by the thousand,
Yet not once in our life repent we one sin.[1]

Yielding to self we sin and know no limit—
What shall we do, O God, how make repentance?

---

[1]   An attempt to reproduce the word-play of the
original, "Bir günaha etmedik hiç bir gün ah".

No one of us but knows his heart's sedition,
Yet we have come, thy mercy to petition.

We hope for grace to make a good profession,
For Mercy's touch, and Ahmed's intercession.

The Refuge in Allah

O God, for sake of him, thy friend, Muhammed,
For sake of Ahmed, rich in intercession,

For sake of Sidre and of highest heaven,
For sake of paths he trod on that high journey,

For sake of noble words on that night spoken,
For eyes which gazed that night upon their Maker,

For sake of light divine and of the Koran,
For Zion's sake, for Kaaba, Merve,[1] Zemzem,

For sake of tears thy lovers shed, unceasing,
For heads and hearts of all thy faithful people,

For hearts aflame with Love's consuming passion,
For mourners weeping blood, so sharp their sorrow,

For slaves who walk thy Way in firm devotion,
For this sure Way, straight to thy presence leading;

What time the span of life on earth is meted,
What time the shades of death must be entreated,

[1]   A hill near Mecca, visited during the annual pilgrimage.

O Holy One, when our last breath doth falter,
Confirm our faith, that it nor change nor alter.

Absolve us, sinful, guilty, rebel creatures,
Free from us sin, that we behold thy features.

Our tombs with Faith's pure light do thou
make splendid,
Our way by cheerful seraph bands attended.

When souls are weighed, our hope in thee we centre;
Guide by thy grace, till Paradise we enter;

Set us near Mustafa, O thou Benignant,
In gardens where there blows no wind malignant;

Then graciously thy face to us revealing,
Content our every wish beyond appealing.

Forgive our rebel deeds, thy mercy hasten,
For Ahmed's sake, our sins but lightly chasten.

Join us to those with whom thou art contented,
Nor gather us among the souls tormented.

May Süleyman, the lowly, find salvation,
Make faith his guide and Paradise his station.

Almighty God, from evil now deliver!
Amen, say all who hope in God the Giver.

A hundred thousand blessings, morn and even,
To Mustafa's pure soul by God be given.

May all his clan, companions and his nation,
His friends and comrades share this acceptation.

May he, our Advocate, reject us never!
May God be gracious to you all for ever!

If from Hell's flame you hope to find salvation,
With love and grief repeat the Salutation.

RESPONSE

Blessing and greeting upon thee, O Apostle of Allah!
Blessing and greeting upon thee, O Beloved of Allah!

The Prayer

Praise and thanks be unto thee, O Lord God. Accept in thy courts of glory this recitation of the Mevlidi Sherif and of the glorious Koran, given in honour of thy noble Friend (prayers and peace be upon him), O Lord God.

We make a gift of the merit and reward of this recitation to the honoured soul of our Master and Prophet ; accept it, we pray thee, O Lord God. We make a gift of it to the souls of all the apostles, to their companions and descendants, to the souls of the saints and of all true Believers ; accept it on their behalf, O Lord God.

Let thy mercy rejoice all the spirits of such as are departed from among the friends who have been responsible for this recitation of the Mevlidi Sherif, O Lord God. Especially the souls of . . . . (Here the leader reads the names of those for the repose of whose souls the recitation has been made, if this has been a service of that nature.) Grant long life to those who remain, O Lord God.

Make the government of our Republic victorious over all its enemies by land, sea and air, O Lord God. Make our beloved land and nation fortunate and happy, O Lord God.

When life comes to an end, may the peace of the Faith be ours, and grant us forgiveness and remission of our sins, O Lord God.

Praise be unto God, the Lord of Glory and of the Abstinent, and peace be upon the Apostles, and thanks be unto God, the Lord of the Here and the Hereafter. Amen.

The Fatiha

Praise be unto Allah, the Lord of all creatures, the Most Merciful, the King of the Day of Judgement. Thee do we worship and of Thee do we beg assistance. Direct us in the right way, the way of those to whom Thou hast been gracious; not of those against whom Thou are incensed, nor of those who go astray. Amin.

THE MEVLIDI SHERIF SCORES

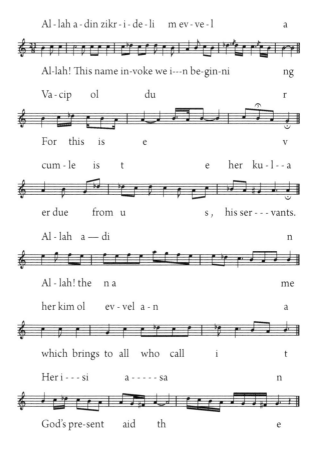

Al-lah a - din zikr - i - de - li m ev - ve - l   a

Al-lah! This name in-voke we i---n be-gin-ni   ng

Va - cip   ol   du   r

For this is   e   v

cum - le is   t   e   her ku - l - - a

er due   from u   s , his ser - - - vants.

Al - lah   a — di   n

Al - lah! the n a   me

her kim ol   ev - vel a - n   a

which brings to all who call   i   t

Her i - - - si   a - - - - - sa   n

God's pre-sent   aid   th   e

60

'No one can know what Muhammed
means to the Turk unless he is
familiar with this poem'

~

Printed in Great Britain
by Amazon